SUPER**SCIENCE**
INFOGRAPHICS

ENERGY AND WAVES THROUGH INFOGRAPHICS

Rebecca Rowell

graphics by
Alex Sciuto

Lerner Publications Company
Minneapolis

Lerner Publications Company
A division of Lerner Publishing Group, Inc.
241 First Avenue North
Minneapolis, MN U.S.A. 55401

Website address: www.lernerbooks.com

Main text set in Univers LT Std 12/15.
Typeface provided by Adobe Systems.

Rowell, Rebecca.
    Energy and waves through infographics / by Rebecca Rowell.
       pages   cm — (Super science infographics)
    Includes index.
    ISBN 978–1–4677–1290–3 (lib. bdg. : alk. paper)
    ISBN 978–1–4677–1785–4 (eBook)
    1. Power resources—Juvenile literature. 2. Electromagnetic waves—Juvenile literature. I. Title.
    TJ163.23.R693 2014
    621.042—dc23   2013004391

Manufactured in the United States of America
1 – BP – 7/15/13

CONTENTS

Introduction
POWER-*FULL*

Do you have a future full of energy and power? To find out, take this test.

1. Do you like to go for swims in hot springs?

2. Do you check the lightbulbs when you visit your friend's house?

3. Do you ever wonder how old the sunlight is?

4. Do you try to split atoms in your spare time?

Did you answer yes to any of those questions?

CONGRATULATIONS!

You could be a budding energy engineer—a scientist who is an expert on energy and its uses. There are many kinds of energy experts. You could focus on solar energy (from the sun), geothermal energy (from Earth's core), or fossil fuels (from ancient plants and creatures). There are even more energy sources to explore. The world is a power-*full* place!

Are you curious yet? Energy is all around you. You can't see it, but there's lots of data to show it. Becoming an expert means sorting through all that data. Scientists use graphs, charts, and other infographics to help sort through all the information. These graphics can make big, mysterious ideas a bit clearer. Are you ready to join in the fun? Let's get started!

INDESTRUCTIBLE ENERGY

It can fly through space! It has unlimited strength! And it can never be destroyed—*ever*! What is this indestructible super being? It's energy. It's the superhero of nature.

Energy cannot be destroyed, but it is always changing. Much of our energy starts with the sun. Then it changes forms. That's how we get things done—by changing one kind of energy into another. Here's one way the sun's energy is transformed into electricity.

The water rushes down the river. It falls down a large waterfall.

During storms, water falls back down to Earth. This makes the water level rise in a river.

A hydroelectric dam is on the river. The dam stops most of the water but lets some out through a tunnel.

The sun's light energy reaches Earth. Light energy warms water on Earth's surface, causing water to evaporate into the air.

Electricity charges the battery in your iPad. Electricity becomes mechanical energy that makes the device work.

The spinning turbines power a generator. The generator makes electricity. The electricity is sent to homes through power lines.

The water rushes through the tunnel. The water turns turbines in the dam.

TWO-SIDED ENERGY

potential energy

kinetic energy

kinetic energy

All energy has two forms. Potential energy is stored energy. It's available to be used. Kinetic energy is energy that is being put to work. Just think about riding a bike. You use kinetic energy to ride up a hill. At the top of the hill, you have potential energy. You're about to fly down that hill. When you do, you use kinetic energy again.

THE ULTIMATE TRAVELER

Light is a pro at traveling. It does it all the time. In fact, every bit of sunlight you see has traveled through space and time to get to Earth. The sunlight seen on Earth was created long ago on the sun. Light makes that important trip at an incredible speed: 186,000 miles (300,000 kilometers) per second. Without sunlight, life on Earth would not exist. Here's how the sun's vital energy makes its way to your front yard.

323,000 miles (520,000 km) thousands of years

SUN'S CORE

1 minute   2 minutes

1. Photons are made inside the superhot core of the sun. A photon is a particle of light.

2. As it moves from the core, the photon bounces against other particles. This makes the journey take a long time. It can take thousands of years for the photon to reach the chromosphere, the outer layer of the sun.

CHROMOSPHERE

Think about it. The light energy that makes your green grass grow was created thousands of years ago in the sun's core. Pretty amazing!

93 million miles
(150 million km)
8 minutes

| minutes | 4 minutes | 5 minutes | 6 minutes | 7 minutes | 8 minutes |

3. Once it escapes the sun, the photon's journey speeds up incredibly. It takes just eight minutes for the photon to make its 93-million-mile journey to Earth.

SO DECOMPOSED!

Imagine a time of hot and muggy weather all over Earth. Swamps covered the land, which was filled with giant ferns and towering trees. Massive insects soared in the skies. And the ocean was bursting with sea life. This was the Carboniferous period on Earth, around 300 million years ago. It is the reason why we have coal, oil, and natural gas today. Here's how those ancient organisms decomposed into fossil fuels.

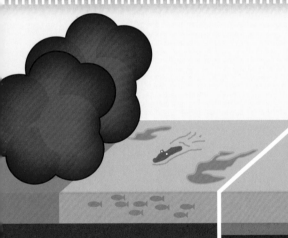

1

Plants and animals thrived in the Carboniferous period.

2

As plants and animals died, their bodies settled at the bottom of swamps, lakes, and oceans. They decomposed and were covered with sand, mud, and rock.

3

Millions of years passed. The layer of plants and animals was covered with more and more mud, rock and sand. Sometimes oceans formed over the layer. The layer was buried hundreds or thousands of feet below Earth's surface.

4

Many more millions of years passed. Pressure from the sand, mud, and rock changed the decomposing material. Heat from Earth and the sun changed the layer too.

5

The decomposed plants and animals turned into fossil fuels over time. Trees, ferns, and other plants became coal. Creatures that lived in the water became oil and natural gas.

6

To reach the buried fossil fuels in modern times, we drill down through layers of land or seafloor. Then pumps bring up the natural gas or oil. To reach coal, we dig deep mines into the ground. Then the coal is dug out and brought up to the surface.

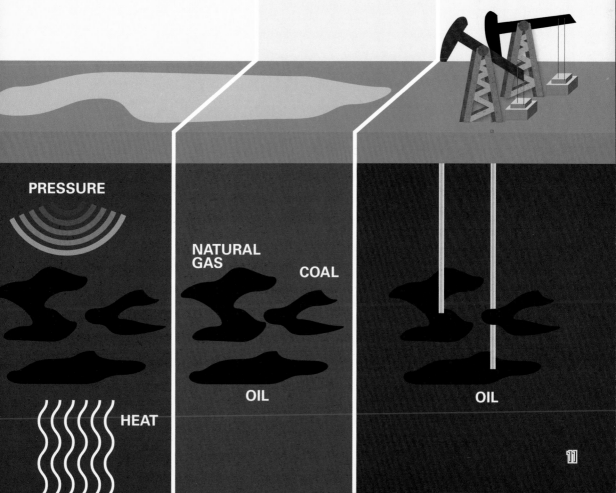

PRESSURE

NATURAL GAS

COAL

OIL

HEAT

OIL

ON THE GRID

Whether you know it or not, you're living on the grid. No, it's not some futuristic world made by robots. The grid is how power gets to your home. It is a series of devices that makes electricity usable for the things we need to power. Here is how the grid works.

2. TRANSMISSION SUBSTATION

Here the electricity is transformed. The force of the electrical current, called voltage, is made higher. This makes it travel long distances better.

3. TRANSMISSION GRID

The electricity moves along high-voltage lines on wire towers. The lines connect to other towers. Electricity can travel in all directions.

1. POWER PLANT

This is where electricity is made. Power can come from all kinds of sources, including the wind, the sun, fossil fuels, and water.

THE SMART GRID

The U.S. power grid is aging. The grid gets overloaded and shuts down in spots. This makes blackouts happen. The smart grid, being built now in some states, is the grid of the future. Here are its features:

- It has a two-way connection from a customer back to the grid. Information about a home's power usage flows back to power stations.

- Power made from a home's solar panels, wind turbines, or other sources can flow onto the grid.

- It can better take energy from renewable sources, such as wind farms.

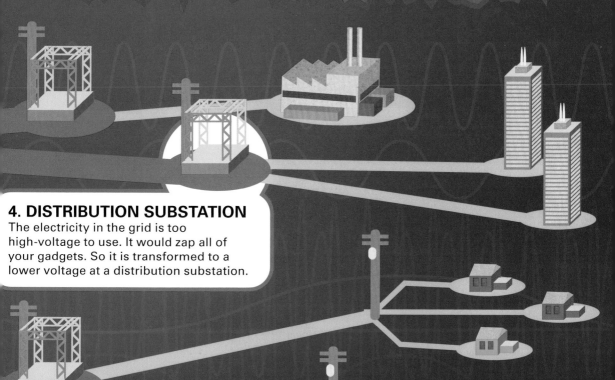

4. DISTRIBUTION SUBSTATION
The electricity in the grid is too high-voltage to use. It would zap all of your gadgets. So it is transformed to a lower voltage at a distribution substation.

5. POLE-TOP TRANSFORMERS
Right before electricity goes to a house or a building, the voltage is lowered again. This is done in a device on an electrical pole.

THE AMAZING EVOLVING LIGHTBULB

It was an amazingly bright idea—turning electricity into light. First came the popular bulb made by Thomas Edison. Its basic design has been used for decades. But lightbulbs have come a long way since that invention. Today's lightbulbs are a lot smarter. They burn longer and use less energy. And each version makes light in a different way. Take a look at how the amazing lightbulb has evolved.

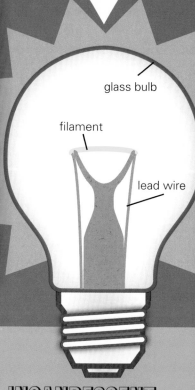

glass bulb

filament

lead wire

INCANDESCENT LIGHTBULB

The filament glows and makes light when electricity passes through it. But 90 percent of the electricity is released as heat.

- ⚡ **60 W**
- 🕐 **1,000 hours**
- 🌡 **90 percent lost**
- $ **4.80**

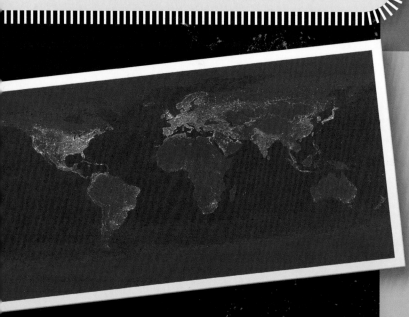

THAT'S BRILLIANT!

We have so many lights now that Earth glows in space. Satellite photos show lit-up areas across the globe. The brightest are major cities. But some spots remain dark, including Antarctica, deep jungle areas in South America, and deserts in Africa.

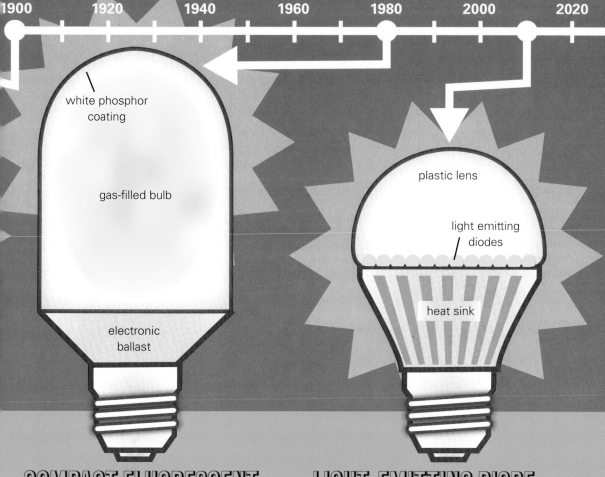

Timeline: 1900 · 1920 · 1940 · 1960 · 1980 · 2000 · 2020

white phosphor coating

gas-filled bulb

electronic ballast

plastic lens

light emitting diodes

heat sink

COMPACT FLUORESCENT (CFL) LIGHTBULB

This bulb lasts 10 times longer than an incandescent bulb! Electricity heats a gas in the bulb, and it emits radiation. A coating absorbs the radiation. This makes light.

- ⚡ **15 W**
- 🕐 **10,000 hours**
- 🌡 **80 percent lost**
- $ **1.20**

LIGHT-EMITTING DIODE (LED) BULB

Diodes in these bulbs conduct electricity. The motion of electrons through the diodes releases photons. This gives off light. An LED bulb lasts 25 times longer than an incandescent bulb.

- ⚡ **12 W**
- 🕐 **25,000 hours**
- 🌡 **10 percent lost**
- $ **1.00**

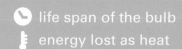

🕐 life span of the bulb $ cost of bulb per year

🌡 energy lost as heat   ⚡ electricity used in watts (W)

*Data is based on two hours of usage each day at a rate of 11 cents per kilowatt.

SPLITTING ATOMS

Some of the smallest particles on Earth can create great amounts of energy. Atoms are the tiny powerhouses of the energy world. When certain atoms are split, it sets off an energy chain reaction called fission. Fission is used in nuclear power plants. Take a look at how it all happens.

ENERGY

neutron

1. A neutron is captured by the uranium 235 nucleus. This makes the nucleus unstable.

3. Neutrons and energy are released from the splitting process. Other by-products are also made.

neutron

neutron

Uranium 235 Nucleus
The nucleus contains neutrons and protons.

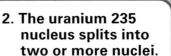 neutrons protons

nuclei

2. The uranium 235 nucleus splits into two or more nuclei.

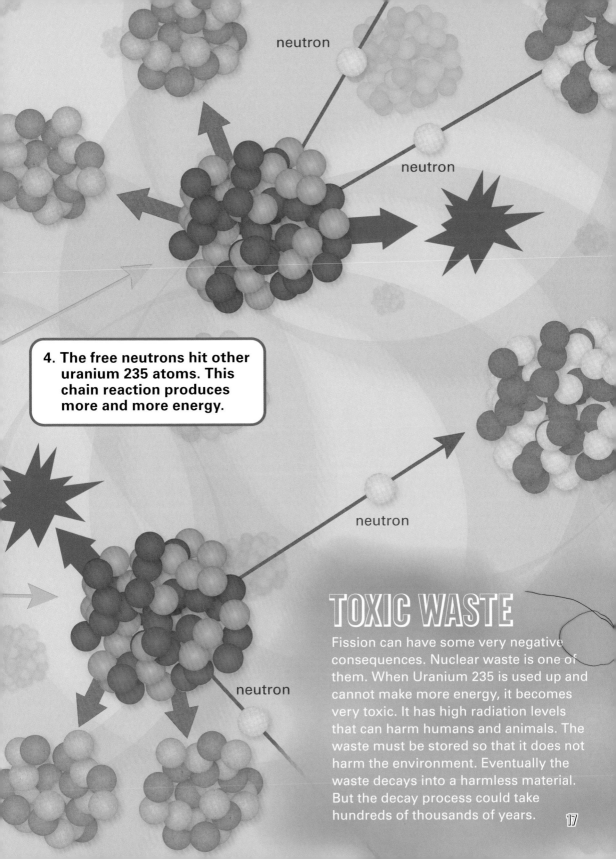

neutron

neutron

4. The free neutrons hit other uranium 235 atoms. This chain reaction produces more and more energy.

neutron

neutron

TOXIC WASTE

Fission can have some very negative consequences. Nuclear waste is one of them. When Uranium 235 is used up and cannot make more energy, it becomes very toxic. It has high radiation levels that can harm humans and animals. The waste must be stored so that it does not harm the environment. Eventually the waste decays into a harmless material. But the decay process could take hundreds of thousands of years.

Onsbjerg Heating Plant

Burns straw from farms on the island to heat the 76 homes in the village of Onsbjerg.

Tanderup Windmills

These windmills make electricity. Each makes enough to power 630 homes each year.

Tranebjerg Heating Plant

Burns straw from farms on the island to make heat for 400 consumers in and near the village of Tranebjerg.

Offshore Windmills

Large offshore windmills make electricity. The power offsets the fossil fuels used for some of the vehicles on the island.

Tanderup

Onsbjerg

Permelille

Tranebjerg

Brundby

Ballen

Brundby/Ballen Heating Plant

Burns straw from farms on the island to make heat for 232 consumers in the villages of Brundby and Ballen.

Brundby Windmills

These windmills make electricity. Each makes enough to power 630 homes each year.

Permelille Windmills

These windmills make electricity. Each makes enough to power 630 homes each year.

THE ENERGY ISLAND

It's a fact: Fossil fuels *will* run out. Renewable energy won't. One Danish island decided to produce only renewable energy. It made the switch in 1997. By 2001 it was using half the fossil fuels it had been using just four years earlier. By 2030 the island plans to be completely fossil fuel–free. Here's how the island of Samsø uses wind, biomass, and the sun to power its 5,000-person community.

Nordby/Mårup Heating Plant

Burns wood chips made on the island and uses solar energy to provide heating for the 178 consumers in the villages of Nordby and Mårup.

Nordby

Mårup

Europe

Denmark

United Kingdom

Finland

Megawatt/hours produced each year by windmills on Samsø

80,000
70,000
60,000
50,000
40,000
30,000
20,000
10,000

TRAVELING SOUND

Sound energy likes to travel. It really can't sit still. It moves through air, water, wood, or other substances. And it all starts with a vibration. Once that vibration gets going, a sound energy wave can go far. Some sounds travel miles before they run out of energy. Sound moving through water travels farther than through the air. Here are some of the long-distance sound travelers of our world.

	100 miles (161 km)	200 miles (322 km)

HOWLER MONKEY
3 MILES (5 KM)

ELEPHANT
6 MILES (10 KM)

DOLPHIN
0.12 MILES (0.19 KM)

BLUE WHALE
500 MILES (805 KM)

BLOOP, 3,107 MILES (5,000 KM)
A mysterious sound that scientists believe comes from icebergs cracking.

SO WHAT EXACTLY ARE SOUND WAVES?

Sound travels, but how does it get where it's going? In waves. These waves have different qualities.

Wavelength

Amplitude

Like an ocean wave, a sound wave has high and low points. A wavelength is the distance from one high point to the next high point or from one low point to the next.

Frequency has to do with pitch. A high-frequency sound has a short wavelength and a high pitch. A low-frequency sound has a longer wavelength.

Amplitude is how loud or quiet a sound is. Louder sounds are shown as taller waves.

300 miles
(483 km)

400 miles
(644 km)

500 miles
(805 km)

THE HEAT UNDERNEATH

There's a lot going on under your feet. Earth's core is a hot, energy-radiating machine. Did you know we can tap that energy for our use? It's called geothermal power. Nothing has to be burned—it's a clean source of energy. And it's abundant and ready to be used 24 hours a day.

A geothermal heat pump uses the constant temperature of the ground about 10 feet (3 meters) down to heat or cool a home. Depending on where you live, this temperature stays between 45°F and 75°F (7°C and 24°C). Here's how you can tap into geothermal energy to heat your home. In the summer, the system can work the opposite way to cool the home.

1

A looping system of pipes is buried below the ground freezing line under your house. At this level, they stay at a constant temperature, never freezing or getting too hot. The pipes link to a heat pump inside the house.

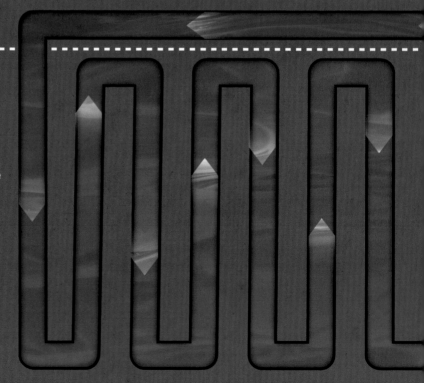

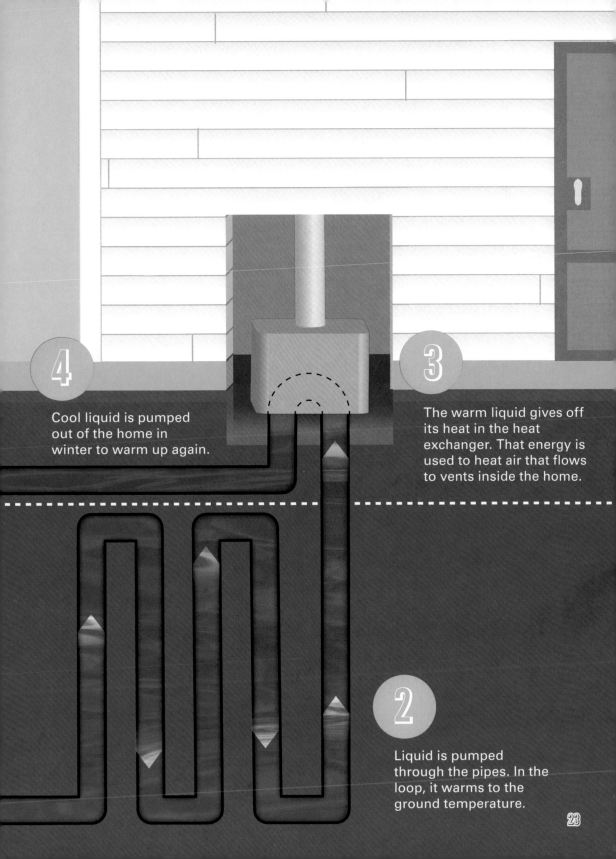

4 Cool liquid is pumped out of the home in winter to warm up again.

3 The warm liquid gives off its heat in the heat exchanger. That energy is used to heat air that flows to vents inside the home.

2 Liquid is pumped through the pipes. In the loop, it warms to the ground temperature.

SUPERPOWER

The United States is a powerful country. It's also a huge power consumer. Cars, planes, heating, and computers—it all takes energy. Americans use so much that it is measured in quadrillions of units (1 quadrillion being 1,000,000,000,000,000). Each unit is called a BTU. Here's what we used by type in quadrillion BTUs and percentages of the total energy used by the United States in 2011.

WHAT WAS ALL THAT ENERGY USED FOR?

Transportation
28%

Homes
22%

Industrial
factories, construction, mining, and other manufacturing companies
31%

Commercial
stores, restaurants, hotels, and other businesses
19%

PETROLEUM
35.3 BTU (36%)

COAL
19.7 BTU (20%)

UNITED STATES ENERGY USE IN 2011

NATURAL GAS
24.8 BTU (26%)

NUCLEAR
8.3 BTU (8%)

RENEWABLE ENERGY
9.1 BTU (9%)

25

ENERGY VAMPIRES

People love their gadgets—laptops, cell phones, iPads, and more. Video games too! But did you know that electronic gadgets are energy vampires? Most are plugged in and on standby or in use at all times. This means those gadgets use power 24/7. Check out how much electricity your favorite gadgets drink up over a year.

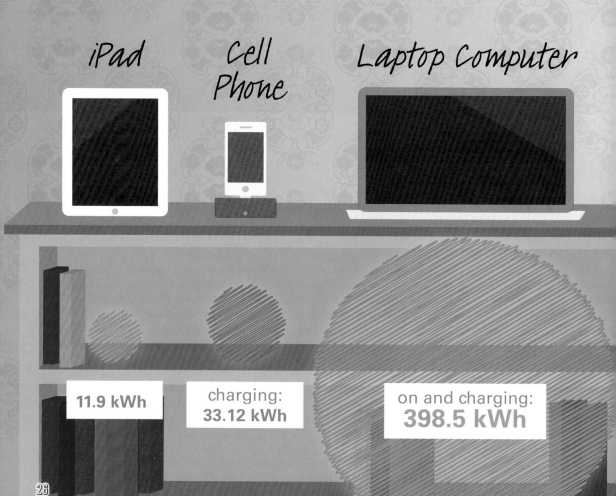

iPad

Cell Phone

Laptop Computer

11.9 kWh

charging:
33.12 kWh

on and charging:
398.5 kWh

KILO-WHAAT??

kWh stands for kilowatt-hour. Electricity is measured in watts. A kilowatt equals 1,000 watts. And a kWh is the amount of energy used by a kilowatt of power in one hour. It is a way to measure electricity use over time.

Video Game Console

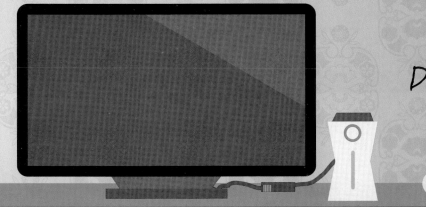

DSL Modem

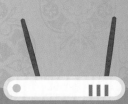

in use: 242.9 kWh
standby: 210.1 kWh

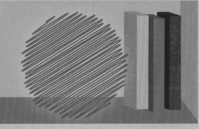
48.33 kWh

TOP TIPS FOR SAVING ENERGY

You've been told a million times. "Turn off the lights. Don't waste electricity!" Wasting energy is expensive. It's bad for the environment too. If less energy is used, less energy has to be made from Earth's resources. What can *you* do? Start with some small changes. They can add up to big differences in our world. Try these simple and easy tips to save energy every day.

LET THE SUNSHINE IN
Turn the lights off and let the sunshine in. Use the sunlight to read instead of a lamp.

TAKE IT OUTSIDE
Get away from your gadgets for a while. Go outside and get moving. You'll save energy and feel better too.

JUST BIKE IT
You don't need to ride in a car to get to the park. Use your bike instead!

SMARTER BULBS
Use CFL or LED lightbulbs. They use much less energy than incandescent bulbs use. And they last much longer.

dance floor

springs

power-generating blocks

JUST DANCE!

You can let off a lot of steam on the dance floor. All that shaking, popping, jumping, and grooving releases energy too! Some club dance floors collect that energy. It's then turned into electricity to power the club. Who knows? Homes of the future may have energy-making floors too. Here's how the dance floors work:

1. Under the dance floor are special springs and power-generating blocks. The dance floor bounces up and down as people dance above.

2. The dance floor pushes down on the blocks. Crystals inside make small electrical charges.

3. The electrical current moves into batteries near the dance floor.

4. The batteries power other parts of the club. As people keep dancing, the batteries are constantly recharged.

That's some fun power!

Glossary

ATOM: the smallest part of something that can exist alone

BIOMASS: plant and animal material used for fuel. Biomass is a renewable resource.

ELECTRICITY: energy in the form of electric current that can occur naturally as lightning or can be produced. Power plants create electricity using different resources.

ELECTRON: part of an atom that has a negative charge and moves around the atom's nucleus. Electrons make electricity possible.

EVAPORATE: to change a liquid to a gas by adding heat to the atoms. The sun makes water evaporate from Earth's surface.

FISSION: breaking apart the nucleus of atoms to release energy. Nuclear energy relies on the fission of uranium 235.

FOSSIL FUEL: an energy source that developed from the remains of animals and plants. Oil, natural gas, and coal are fossil fuels.

GEOTHERMAL: having to do with heat from Earth. Some people heat their homes with geothermal energy.

INDESTRUCTIBLE: not able to be destroyed. Energy is indestructible.

KINETIC ENERGY: energy that is already working; it's in action. A moving hammer or a spinning windmill are types of kinetic energy.

NUCLEAR ENERGY: energy released by splitting the nucleus of an atom. Nuclear energy is not renewable because it relies on uranium, a finite material.

POTENTIAL ENERGY: energy that is stored and waiting to be used. A stretched spring is one type of potential energy.

RADIATION: energy that is released in rays from an object, such as heat or light. Gas in a CFL lightbulb emits radiation.

RENEWABLE: able to be replaced; this type of energy comes from sources such as the sun and wind that won't run out. Renewable energy is cleaner than energy from fossil fuels.

SOUND: vibration of air or other molecules. Sound travels in waves.

TURBINE: an engine that is powered by water, steam, or gas that passes through a wheel. A turbine is used in a hydroelectric dam.

Further Information

Challoner, Jack. *Energy*. New York: DK Publishing, 2012.
This book tells the story of energy.

Electrical Energy Cost Calculator
http://www.csgnetwork.com /elecenergycalcs.html
This online tool can give you an idea of how much energy we consume using and doing everyday things.

Energy Kids
http://www.eia.gov/kids/energy .cfm?page=natural_gas_home -basics
This site from the U.S. Energy Information Administration has information about renewable and nonrenewable fuels.

Energy Quest
http://energyquest.ca.gov/index .html
Learn the story of energy, including its forms and nonrenewable and renewable sources. Meet some super scientists too!

Fridell, Ron. *Earth-Friendly Energy*. Minneapolis: Lerner Publications, 2009.
Learn about renewable energy sources, including solar and wind power.

Gardner, Robert. *Light, Sound, and Waves Science Fair Projects*. Berkeley Heights, NJ: Enslow, 2010.
You don't need to participate in a science fair to make a cool project about energy. Experiments in this book explore light, sound, and other waves using simple materials.

Horn, Geoffrey M. *Coal, Oil, and Natural Gas*. New York: Chelsea Clubhouse, 2010.
Explore fossil fuels, including where they come from, how we use them, and their future.

Masters, Nancy R. *How Did That Get to My House? Natural Gas*. Ann Arbor, MI: Cherry Lake Publishing, 2009.
Curious about how natural gas makes its way to your home? This book has the answers.

Riley, Peter D. *Sound*. Mankato, MN: Sea-to-Sea Publications, 2011.
Learn to use the scientific method to investigate sound and hearing in this book by a former teacher.

Walker, Sally M. *Investigating Electricity*. Minneapolis: Lerner Publications, 2011.
You use electricity every day. Learn about the valuable resource in this book.

LERNER SOURCE
Expand learning beyond the printed book. Download free, complementary educational resources for this book from our website, www.lerneresource.com.

Index

PHOTO ACKNOWLEDGMENTS:
Additional images used in this book are used with the permission of: U.S.
Air Force photo by Edward Aspera Jr., p. 6 (top); © David Iliff/Dreamstime.
com, p. 6 (bottom left); Bureau of Reclamation, p. 6 (bottom right); Chris Gin/
Wikimedia Commons, p. 7 (top left); Jim Henderson/Wikimedia Commons,
p. 7 (top right); Tony Boon/Wikimedia Commons, p. 7 (middle); Jon Sullivan/
Wikimedia Commons, p. 7 (bottom); Craig Mayhew and Robert Simmon,
NASA GSFC, p. 14.